# Weather

**Written by Jenny Feely**
Series Consultant: Linda Hoyt

**WorldWise**
Content-based Learning

# Contents

# Introduction

Weather changes every day. It can be warm or cool, or very hot or cold.

It can also bring storms and **heat waves**. All types of weather are caused by changes in the air around us.

# Chapter 1

# Wind, clouds and rain

The earth is surrounded by a layer of air called the **atmosphere**. When the sun warms the air in the atmosphere, the warm air rises and pushes cooler air aside. This creates wind.

As the sun warms water on the land, the water dries up and forms **clouds**.

The mix of wind and clouds makes different kinds of weather.

## What is wind?

Wind is moving air. A gentle, slow wind is called a **breeze,** and a strong, fast wind is called a gale.

**Gale-force** winds can rip trees out of the ground and blow buildings over.

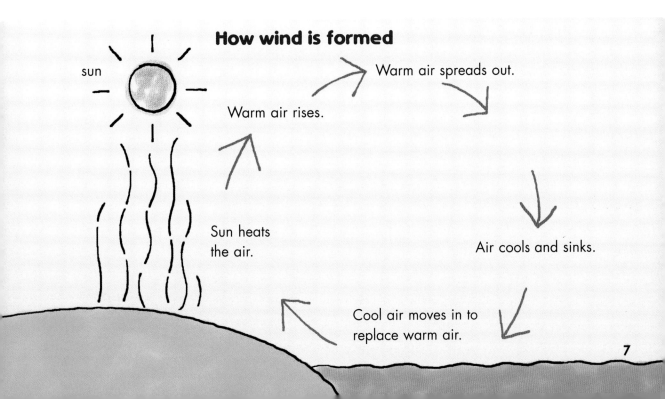

### How wind is formed

sun

Warm air spreads out.

Warm air rises.

Sun heats the air.

Air cools and sinks.

Cool air moves in to replace warm air.

# What makes clouds and rain?

Clouds are formed as the sun warms the water in rivers, lakes and oceans. Some of the water turns from a liquid into a gas that rises into the air. This is called evaporation.

When evaporated water cools, it turns back into tiny droplets that form clouds. In the clouds, the droplets join with other droplets and fall to the ground as rain, hail or snow.

## The water cycle

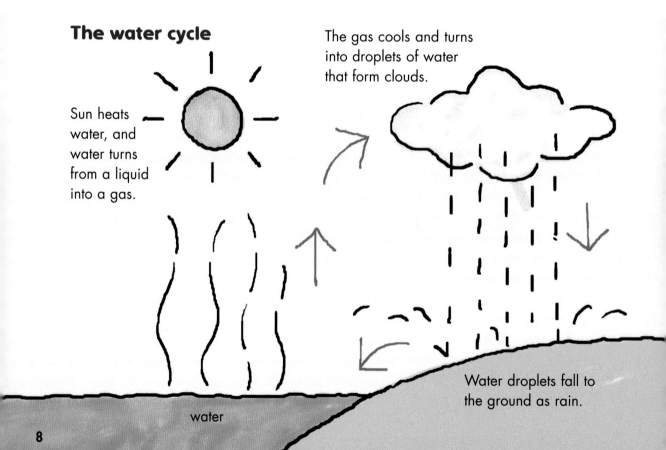

The gas cools and turns into droplets of water that form clouds.

Sun heats water, and water turns from a liquid into a gas.

Water droplets fall to the ground as rain.

water

## Find out more

What happens when there is too much rain or not enough rain?

# Chapter 2

# Cold weather

Most of the time, cold weather is not a problem, but if the **temperature** becomes too cold, the weather can become very dangerous.

When it is very cold, water in **clouds** can become snow, hail, fog or frost.

## Snow

Sometimes, water droplets in clouds freeze and form tiny **crystals** that fall to the ground as snow. Snowflakes have many different shapes.

## Hail

Hail is also formed in very cold air.  Hail
forms when wind makes droplets of water
move up and down in a cloud.  This makes
them melt and freeze again and again until
they become balls of ice that
fall to the ground.

## Fog

Fog happens when clouds form close to the ground.  Fog makes it difficult to see.  Planes, boats, and cars cannot safely move in thick fog.

Fog usually disappears when the sun warms the air and **evaporates** the water in the clouds, or when wind blows it away.

# Dew and frost

Dew is made up of tiny drops of water. It is found first thing in the morning when everything outside is wet even though it has not rained.

Frost is frozen dew. It forms when the air is very cold.

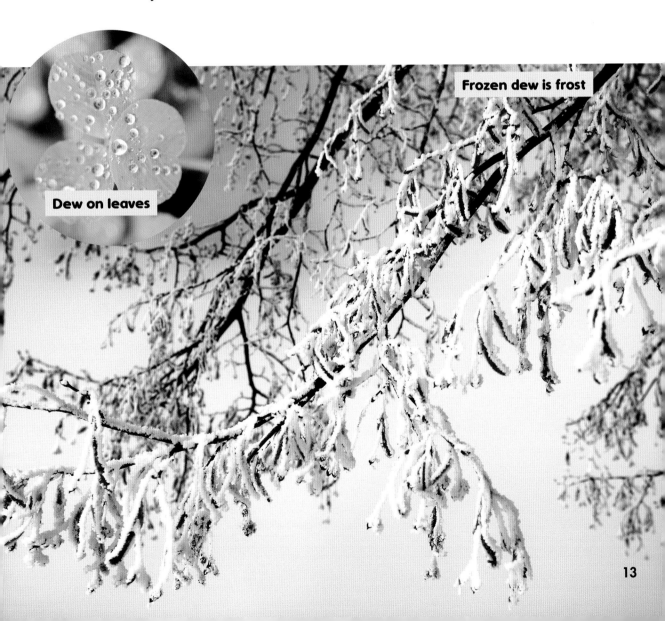

Frozen dew is frost

Dew on leaves

# Chapter 3

# Storms

During storms, the weather becomes very wild, with strong winds and lots of rain, hail or snow. There can also be thunder and lightning. Sometimes, storms bring a huge amount of rain, snow or hail.

Storms can cause a lot of damage to houses, and other buildings and farmland.

# Dust storms

Dust storms happen when strong winds blow over dry land. The winds pick up small pieces of dirt and dust, and blow them across the land in **clouds**. Dust storms can darken the daytime and make it impossible to see what is nearby.

**Did you know?**
When dust storms twirl around and around, they are called dust devils.

# Sandstorms

Sandstorms form in deserts when strong winds pick up lots of sand and blow it across the land. Sandstorms are very dangerous. They can bury whole buildings. People caught in sandstorms must cover their faces and seek shelter.

15

## Thunderstorms

A thunderstorm happens when warm air and cool air crash together. This causes electricity to form in the air.

When the electricity moves down to the ground, it gives off a bright flash of light called lightning. Thunder is the rumbling noise lightning makes as it moves through the air.

When lightning hits the ground, it can cause fires or explosions. People can be hurt or even killed if lightning hits them.

## Tornadoes

Tornadoes are funnels of very strong wind that sometimes form in thunderstorms.

Tornadoes move very quickly across the ground, sucking up everything in their path.  They can destroy buildings and rip up trees.

## Cyclones

Cyclones are very dangerous storms.
They can destroy whole towns and kill people.

Cyclones are formed by the movement of warm and cool air in the **atmosphere**.

During a cyclone, the air spins very quickly in a huge circle, bringing powerful winds and rain.  The spinning air in the cyclone can also cause the sea to flood the land.

# Conclusion

Weather is always changing. Sometimes, it is warm and comfortable. At other times, it is wild and dangerous. All these changes in the weather are caused by the sun heating the water and air, which causes the air to move around the earth.

# Glossary

**atmosphere**   the layer of air that surrounds the earth

**breeze**   a gentle wind

**clouds**   collections of tiny water drops that are too small to fall to Earth

**crystals**   small pieces of ice that have a symmetrical shape

**evaporation**   to change from being a liquid into a gas

**gale-force**   a strong wind that has gusts between 63 and 87 kilometres per hour

**heat waves**   a number of days in a row where the weather is extremely hot

**temperature**   the amount of heat in the air

# Index